NURSERY RHYMES

Mother Goose

MOTHER GOOSE RHYMES

TICKTOCK

TIME NURSERY RHYMES

compiled by Terry Pierce ∿ illustrated by Cori Doerrfeld

PICTURE WINDOW BOOKS
Minneapolis, Minnesota

Special thanks to our advisers for their expertise:

Terry Flaherty, Ph.D., Professor of English
Minnesota State University, Mankato

Susan Kesselring, M.A., Literacy Educator
Rosemount–Apple Valley–Eagan (Minnesota) School District

Editors: Christianne Jones and Dodie Marie Miller
Designer: Tracy Davies
Page Production: Angela Kilmer
Art Director: Nathan Gassman
The illustrations in this book were created digitally.

Editor's Note: Editorial and formatting decisions for most
of the nursery rhymes in this book were based on the
following source: *The Random House Book of Mother
Goose* (1986), selected and illustrated by Arnold Lobel.

Picture Window Books
5115 Excelsior Boulevard
Suite 232
Minneapolis, MN 55416
877-845-8392
www.picturewindowbooks.com

Library of Congress Cataloging-in-Publication Data
Pierce, Terry.
Ticktock : time nursery rhymes / compiled by Terry Pierce ;
illustrated by Cori Doerrfeld.
p. cm. – (Mother Goose rhymes)
Summary: An illustrated collection of twenty nursery
rhymes related to time.
ISBN-13: 978-1-4048-2348-8 (library binding)
ISBN-10: 1-4048-2348-4 (library binding)
ISBN-13: 978-1-4048-2354-9 (paperback)
ISBN-10: 1-4048-2354-9 (paperback)
1. Nursery rhymes. 2. Time–Juvenile poetry. 3. Children's
poetry. [1. Nursery rhymes. 2. Time–Poetry.] I. Doerrfeld,
Cori, ill. II. Mother Goose. Selections. III. Title. IV. Title:
Time nursery rhymes.
PZ8.3.P558643Tic 2006
398.8–dc22 [E]   2006027250

TABLE OF CONTENTS

Nursery Rhymes About Time 5

Hickory, Dickory, Dock 6

The Ten O'Clock Scholar 7

Bell Horses 8

The Cock Crows in the Morn 9

An Apple a Day 10

Cock Robin Got Up Early 12

Dreams 13

Solomon Grundy 14

Awake, Arise 16

Sally Go Round the Sun 17

The Donkey 18

Tommy Snooks 19

John Wesley 20

Elsie Marley Has Grown So Fine 21

I Saw Three Ships 22

Mend My Shoe 24

There Was an Old Woman 25

Play Days 26

Saturday, Sunday 27

A Week of Birthdays 28

The History of Nursery Rhymes and Mother Goose 31

To Learn More 32

Index of First Lines 32

MOTHER
GOO

NURSERY RHYMES ABOUT TIME

I'TS TIME TO WAKE UP! IT'S TIME FOR SCHOOL! IT'S TIME TO PLAY! You can tell time with a clock. You can also tell time by days, weeks, and months. There are lots of nursery rhymes about time. **Can you find a rhyme about your favorite time of the day?**

HICKORY, DICKORY, DOCK

Hickory, dickory, dock,
The mouse ran up the clock.
The clock struck one,
Down the mouse did run.
Hickory, dickory, dock.

THE TEN O'CLOCK SCHOLAR

A diller, a dollar,

A ten o'clock scholar,

What makes you come so soon?

You used to come at ten o'clock,

But now you come at noon.

BELL HORSES

Bell horses, bell horses,
What time of day?
One o'clock, two o'clock,
Three and away.

8

THE COCK CROWS IN THE MORN

The cock crows in the morn
To tell us to rise,
And he that lies late
Will never be wise:

For early to bed
And early to rise
Is the way to be healthy
And wealthy and wise.

AN APPLE A DAY

An apple a day
Sends the doctor away.

Apple in the morning,
Doctor's warning.

Roast apple at night
Starves the doctor outright.

Eat an apple going to bed,
Knock the doctor on the head.

Three each day, seven days a week,
Ruddy apple, ruddy cheek.

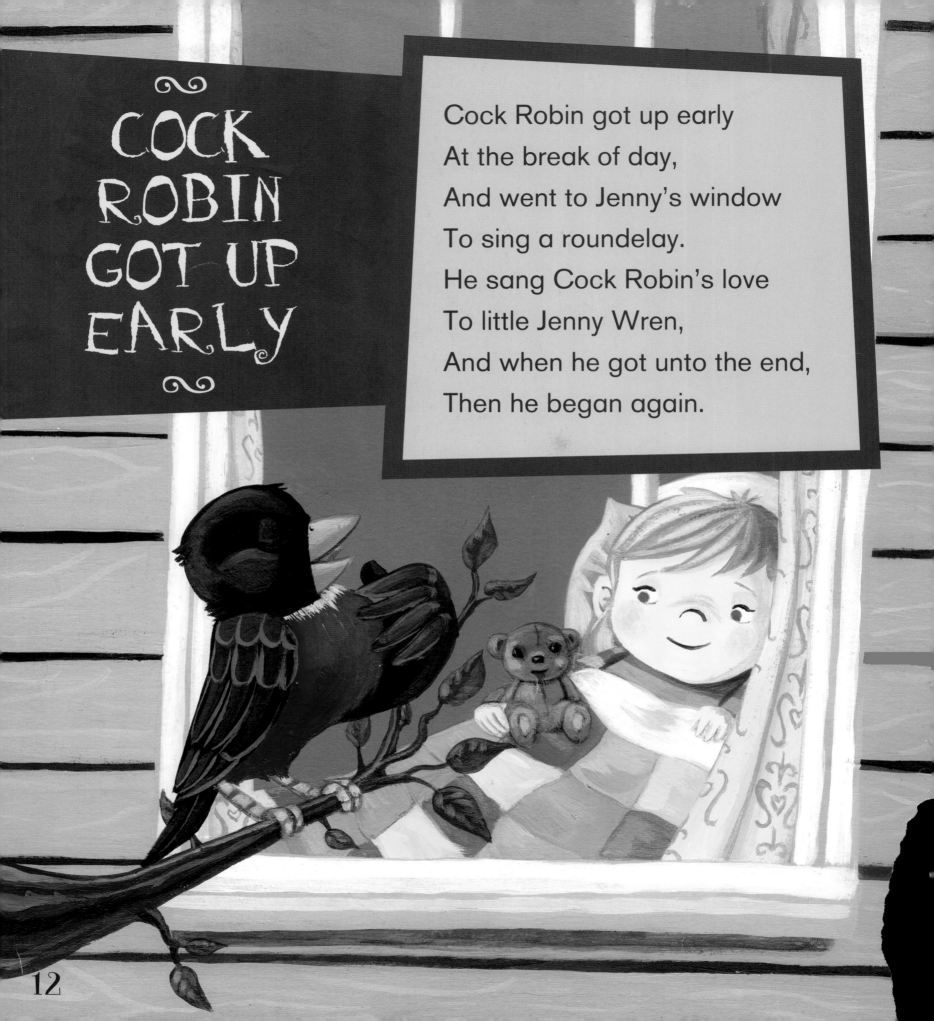

COCK ROBIN GOT UP EARLY

Cock Robin got up early
At the break of day,
And went to Jenny's window
To sing a roundelay.
He sang Cock Robin's love
To little Jenny Wren,
And when he got unto the end,
Then he began again.

Friday night's dream, on Saturday told,
Is sure to come true, be it never so old.

Solomon Grundy

Solomon Grundy,
Born on a Monday,
Christened on Tuesday,
Married on Wednesday,
Took ill on Thursday,
Worse on Friday,
Died on Saturday,
Buried on Sunday.
This is the end
Of Solomon Grundy.

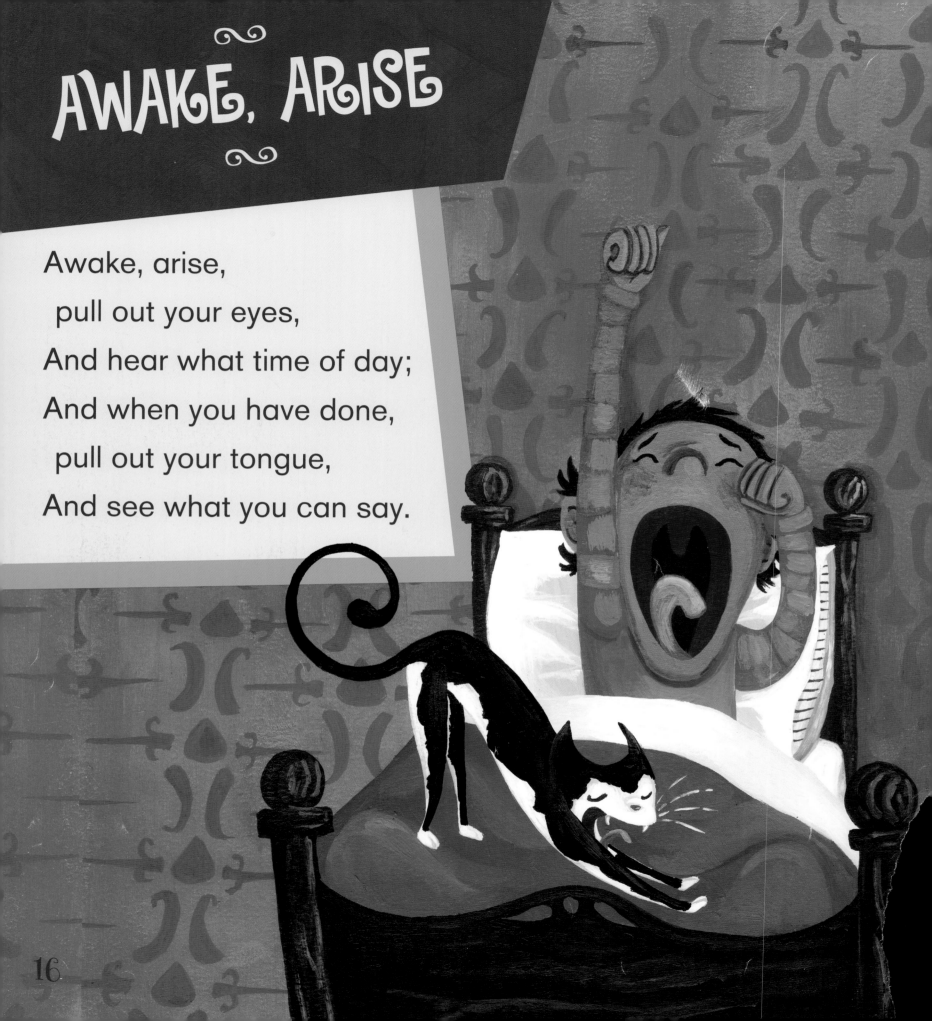

AWAKE, ARISE

Awake, arise,
  pull out your eyes,
And hear what time of day;
And when you have done,
  pull out your tongue,
And see what you can say.

SALLY GO ROUND THE SUN

Sally go round
  the sun,
Sally go round
  the moon,
Sally go round
  the chimney pots
On a Saturday afternoon.

THE DONKEY

Donkey, donkey, old and gray,
Open your mouth and gently bray;
Lift your ears and blow your horn,
To wake the world this sleepy morn.

TOMMY SNOOKS

As Tommy Snooks and Bessy Brooks
Were walking out one Sunday;
Says Tommy Snooks to Bessy Brooks,
"Tomorrow will be Monday."

∾ JOHN WESLEY ∾

There was a man, he had two sons,
And these two sons were brothers.
John Wesley was the name of one,
And Charlie was the other's.

Now these two brothers had a coat,
They bought it on a Monday.
John Wesley wore it all the week,
And Charlie on a Sunday.

ELSIE MARLEY HAS GROWN SO FINE

Elsie Marley has grown so fine,

She won't get up to feed the swine,

But lies in bed till eight or nine,

And surely she does take her time.

I SAW THREE SHIPS

I saw three ships come sailing by,
Come sailing by, come sailing by,
I saw three ships come sailing by,
On New Year's Day in the morning.

And what do you think was in them then,
Was in them then, was in them then?
And what do you think was in them then?
On New Year's Day in the morning?

Three pretty girls were in them then,
Were in them then, were in them then,
Three pretty girls were in them then,
On New Year's Day in the morning.

One could whistle, and one could sing,
And one could play the violin;
Such joy there was at my wedding,
On New Year's Day in the morning.

MEND MY SHOE

Cobbler, cobbler, mend my shoe,
Yes, good master, that I'll do.
Stitch it up and stitch it down,
And then I'll give you half a crown.

Cobbler, cobbler, mend my shoe,
Get it done by half-past two;
Half-past two, it can't be done,
Get it done by half-past one.

THERE WAS AN OLD WOMAN

There was an old woman of Surrey,
Who was morn, noon, and night in a hurry;
Called her husband a fool,
Drove her children to school,
The worrying old woman of Surrey.

PLAY DAYS

How many days has my baby to play?
Saturday, Sunday, Monday,
Tuesday, Wednesday, Thursday, Friday,
Saturday, Sunday, Monday.
Hop away, skip away,
My baby wants to play,
My baby wants to play every day.

On Saturday night shall be all my care

To powder my locks and curl my hair;

On Sunday morning my love will come in,

When he will marry me with a gold ring.

A WEEK OF BIRTHDAYS

Monday's child is fair of face,
Tuesday's child is full of grace,
Wednesday's child is full of woe,
Thursday's child has far to go,
Friday's child is loving and giving,
Saturday's child works hard for his living.
And the child that is born on Sunday
Is bonny and blithe, and good and gay.

THE HISTORY OF NURSERY RHYMES AND
MOTHER GOOSE

Nursery rhymes circulated orally for hundreds of years. In the 18th century, collectors wrote down the rhymes, printed them, and sold them to parents and other adults to help them remember the rhymes so they could share them with children.

Some of these collections were called "Mother Goose" collections. Nobody knows exactly who Mother Goose was (though there are plenty of myths about her), but she was probably a respected storyteller. Occasionally the rhymes commented on real people and events. The meaning of many of the rhymes has been lost, but the catchy rhythms remain.

Mother Goose nursery rhymes have evolved from many sources through time. From the 1600s until now, the appealing rhythms, rhymes, humor, and playfulness found in these verses, stories, and concepts contribute to what readers now know as Mother Goose nursery rhymes.

TO LEARN MORE

AT THE LIBRARY

Crump, Fred. *Mother Goose Nursery Rhymes*. Nashville: Winston-Derek Publishers, 1990.

Kessler, Leonard P. *Hickory Dickory Dock*. Champaign, Ill.: Garrard Pub. Co., 1980.

Lansky, Bruce. *New Rhymes for Playtime*. New York: Simon & Schuster, 1995.

ON THE WEB

FactHound offers a safe, fun way to find Web sites related to this book. All of the sites on FactHound have been researched by our staff.

1. Visit *www.facthound.com*
2. Type in this special code: 1404823484
3. Click on the FETCH IT button.

Your trusty FactHound will fetch the best sites for you!

INDEX OF FIRST LINES

A diller, a dollar, 7
An apple a day, 10
As Tommy Snooks and Bessy Brooks, 19
Awake, arise, 16
Bell horses, bell horses, 8
Cobbler, cobbler, mend my shoe, 24
Cock Robin got up early, 12
Donkey, donkey, old and gray, 18
Elsie Marley has grown so fine, 21
Friday night's dream, on Saturday told, 13
Hickory, dickory, dock, 6
How many days has my baby to play? 26
I saw three ships come sailing by, 22
Monday's child is fair of face, 29
On Saturday night shall be all my care, 27
Sally go round, 17
Solomon Grundy, 14
The cock crows in the morn, 9
There was a man, he had two sons, 20
There was an old woman of Surrey, 25

⌒ LOOK FOR ALL OF THE BOOKS IN THE ⌒ MOTHER GOOSE RHYMES SERIES:

Counting Your Way: Number Nursery Rhymes
Cuddly Critters: Animal Nursery Rhymes
Forecasting Fun: Weather Nursery Rhymes
Friendly Faces: People Nursery Rhymes
Sleepytime: Bedtime Nursery Rhymes
Ticktock: Time Nursery Rhymes

Mother Goose

NURSERY RHYMES